EXPLORE THE UNITED STATES

GEORGIA

Sarah Tieck

Big Buddy Books

An Imprint of Abdo Publishing
abdobooks.com

abdobooks.com

Published by Abdo Publishing, a division of ABDO, PO Box 398166, Minneapolis, Minnesota 55439. Copyright © 2020 by Abdo Consulting Group, Inc. International copyrights reserved in all countries. No part of this book may be reproduced in any form without written permission from the publisher. Big Buddy Books™ is a trademark and logo of Abdo Publishing.

Printed in the United States of America, North Mankato, Minnesota
102019
012020

THIS BOOK CONTAINS RECYCLED MATERIALS

Design: Aruna Rangarajan, Mighty Media, Inc.
Production: Mighty Media, Inc.
Editor: Liz Salzmann

Cover Photograph: iStockphoto
Interior Photographs: Anthony Nesmith/AP Images, p. 18 (inset); AP Images, p. 21; BJOERN SIGURDSON/AP Images, p. 23; Carol M Highsmith/Library of Congress, p. 13; Courtesy Yale University Art Gallery, Yale University, New Haven, Conn./Wikimedia Commons, p. 26 (bottom left); John Bazemore/AP Images, p. 9 (bottom left); ownway/iStockphoto, p. 30 (center); RICK BOWMER/AP Images, p. 27 (bottom); Sean Pavone/iStockphoto, p. 9 (right); Shutterstock Images, pp. 4, 5, 6, 7, 8, 9, 10, 11, 12, 14, 15, 16, 17, 18, 19, 20, 22, 24, 25, 26 (top, bottom right), 27 (top right), 28 (all), 29 (all), 30; Underwood and Underwood, New York/Wikimedia Commons, p. 27 (top left)

Populations figures from census.gov

Library of Congress Control Number: 2019943201

Publisher's Cataloging-in-Publication Data

Names: Tieck, Sarah, author.
Title: Georgia / by Sarah Tieck
Description: Minneapolis, Minnesota : Abdo Publishing, 2020 | Series: Explore the United States | Includes online resources and index.
Identifiers: ISBN 9781532191138 (lib. bdg.) | ISBN 9781532177866 (ebook)
Subjects: LCSH: U.S. states--Juvenile literature. | Southeastern States--Juvenile literature. | Physical geography--United States--Juvenile literature. | Georgia--History--Juvenile literature.
Classification: DDC 975.8--dc23

CONTENTS

One Nation 4

Georgia Up Close 6

Important Cities 8

Georgia in History 12

Across the Land 14

Earning a Living 16

Sports Page 18

Hometown Heroes 20

A Great State 24

Timeline 26

Tour Book 28

Fast Facts 30

Glossary 31

Online Resources 31

Index 32

ONE NATION

The United States is a diverse country. It has farmland, cities, coasts, and mountains. Its people come from many different backgrounds. And, its history covers more than 200 years.

Today the country includes 50 states. Georgia is one of these states. Let's learn more about Georgia and its story!

DID YOU KNOW?

Georgia became a state on January 2, 1788. It was the fourth state to join the nation.

Georgia is known for its peaches. Before peaches grow, the trees are covered in fragrant peach blossoms!

CHAPTER 2

GEORGIA UP CLOSE

The United States has four main regions. Georgia is in the South.

Georgia has five states on its borders. Tennessee and North Carolina are north. Alabama is west. Florida is south. South Carolina and the Atlantic Ocean are east.

Georgia has a total area of 59,425 square miles (153,910 sq km). About 10.5 million people live in the state.

Puerto Rico became a US commonwealth in 1952.

DID YOU KNOW?
Washington, DC, is the US capital city. Puerto Rico is a US commonwealth. This means it is governed by its own people.

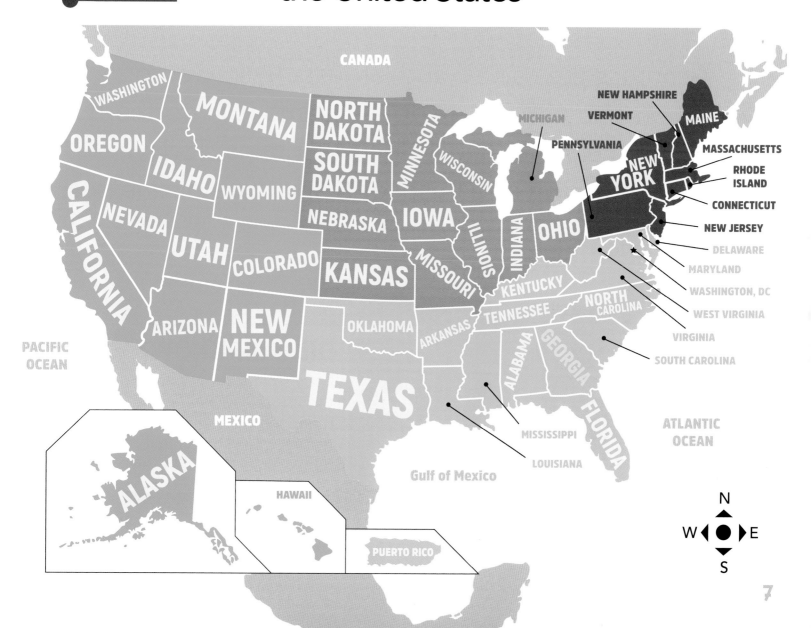

★ Regions of ★
the United States

West
Midwest
South
Northeast

CANADA

WASHINGTON
OREGON
CALIFORNIA
IDAHO
NEVADA
UTAH
ARIZONA
MONTANA
WYOMING
COLORADO
NEW MEXICO
NORTH DAKOTA
SOUTH DAKOTA
NEBRASKA
KANSAS
OKLAHOMA
TEXAS
MINNESOTA
IOWA
MISSOURI
ARKANSAS
WISCONSIN
ILLINOIS
INDIANA
OHIO
KENTUCKY
TENNESSEE
MISSISSIPPI
LOUISIANA
ALABAMA
GEORGIA
FLORIDA
MICHIGAN
NORTH CAROLINA
SOUTH CAROLINA

NEW HAMPSHIRE
VERMONT
MAINE
PENNSYLVANIA
NEW YORK
MASSACHUSETTS
RHODE ISLAND
CONNECTICUT
NEW JERSEY
DELAWARE
MARYLAND
WASHINGTON, DC
WEST VIRGINIA
VIRGINIA

PACIFIC OCEAN

MEXICO

ALASKA

HAWAII

PUERTO RICO

Gulf of Mexico

ATLANTIC OCEAN

N
W E
S

CHAPTER 3

IMPORTANT CITIES

Atlanta is the capital and largest city in Georgia. It is home to 498,044 people. Atlanta is in northern Georgia, near the Blue Ridge Mountains. Today, Atlanta is known as a base for many large businesses.

CNN was founded in 1980.

DID YOU KNOW?

Coca-Cola and CNN are two important companies based in Atlanta. CNN was the first news station to report news 24 hours a day.

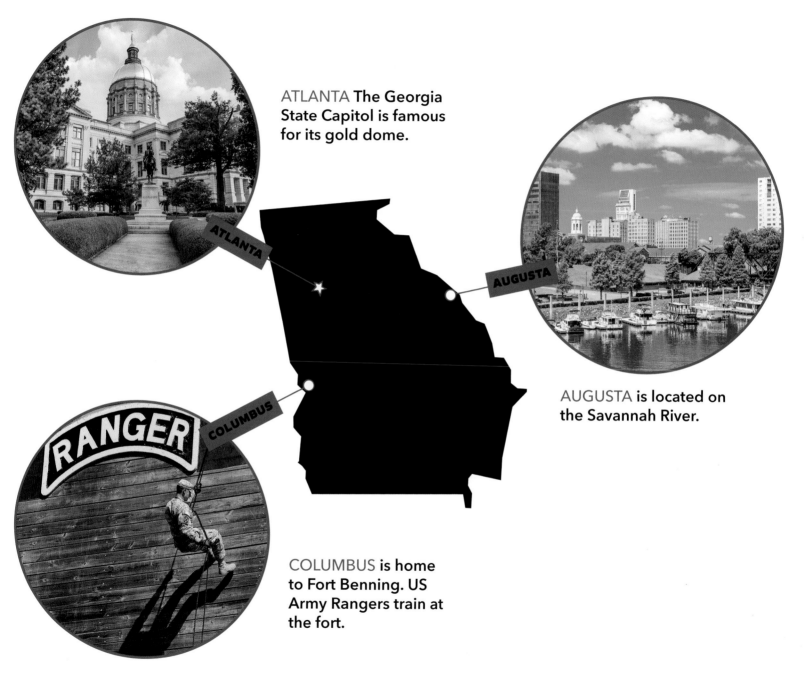

ATLANTA **The Georgia State Capitol is famous for its gold dome.**

AUGUSTA **is located on the Savannah River.**

COLUMBUS **is home to Fort Benning. US Army Rangers train at the fort.**

Piedmont Park is one of
Atlanta's more than 300 parks.

Augusta is Georgia's second-largest city, with 197,166 people. It was a trading post in the 1730s. It was also Georgia's capital from 1786 to 1795.

Columbus is the third-largest city in the state. Its population is 194,160. Columbus is located on the banks of the Chattahoochee River.

DID YOU KNOW?

Columbus has a walking and biking area along the river called the Chattahoochee RiverWalk. It is 22 miles (35 km) long.

CHAPTER 4

GEORGIA IN HISTORY

Georgia's history includes Native Americans, explorers, colonists, and war. Native Americans lived in the area for many years. Then in the 1500s, people from Spain explored and settled there.

In the late 1600s, England gained control of the area. In 1732, Georgia became the thirteenth colony. Its colonists fought against England in the Revolutionary War. Georgia became a state in 1788. Later, Georgia played an important part in the American Civil War.

The flag of the original 13 states

DID YOU KNOW?
Georgia and 12 other colonies helped form the United States.

Several battles took place in Georgia during the American Civil War. In 1864, Atlanta was burned by Northern soldiers.

CHAPTER 5

ACROSS THE LAND

Georgia has hills, forests, and flat, open land. The Blue Ridge Mountains are in northern Georgia. They are part of the Appalachian Mountains. Part of the state's eastern border is lined with beaches.

Many types of animals make their homes in Georgia. These include bears, alligators, and rabbits. Sea turtles swim off the state's coast.

Atlanta is sometimes called "Hotlanta."

DID YOU KNOW?
Georgia has mild weather. Atlanta's average high temperature in August is 88°F (31°C). In January, it is 52°F (11°C).

Forests cover 24,768,000 acres (10,023,254 ha) of Georgia's land.

CHAPTER 6

EARNING A LIVING

Georgia used to be mostly a farming state. Important crops are still grown there. These include cotton, pecans, peanuts, peaches, corn, and melons.

Today, other important businesses operate in Georgia. These include finance, real estate, construction, and transportation businesses. Many people also work in government and manufacturing jobs.

DID YOU KNOW?
Georgia grows about half of the nation's peanuts! So, it is sometimes called the Goober State. Goober is a southern word for peanut.

Georgia's farmers grow more than 130 million pounds (58,967,008 kg) of peaches each year.

CHAPTER 7

SPORTS PAGE

Many people think of sports when they think of Georgia. This state has baseball, football, soccer, and basketball teams. College sports are popular as well.

Georgia is also known for golf. Every April, the US Masters is held in Augusta. Top golfers from around the world play in the Masters.

The Atlanta Dream joined the WNBA in 2008. Angel McCoughtry is a star player on the team.

DID YOU KNOW?

Atlanta is home to Georgia's major sports teams. The Braves play baseball, the Falcons play football, the Atlanta United FC play soccer, and the Hawks play basketball.

Atlanta United FC won the Major League Soccer championship in 2018!

CHAPTER 8

HOMETOWN HEROES

Many famous people are from Georgia. Martin Luther King Jr. was born in Atlanta in 1929. He was a civil rights movement leader. He fought for rights for African Americans.

King won the Nobel Peace Prize in 1964 for his work. He was killed in 1968. Today, Americans honor King with a national holiday.

Martin Luther King Jr. National Historical Park in Atlanta includes King's childhood home.

DID YOU KNOW?
Martin Luther King Jr. Day falls on the third Monday in January.

King gave speeches and led marches. He wanted people of all races to have the same rights.

Jimmy Carter was born in 1924 in Plains, Georgia. In 1971, he became Georgia's governor. He helped African Americans and improved schools. Carter became the thirty-ninth US president in 1977. He served until 1981.

DID YOU KNOW?
Gladys Knight was born in Atlanta in 1944. She became a famous singer and songwriter. She and her group, Gladys Knight & the Pips, are members of the Rock & Roll Hall of Fame!

After serving as president, Carter worked for peace around the world. He won a Nobel Peace Prize for his work in 2002.

CHAPTER 9

A GREAT STATE

The story of Georgia is important to the United States. The people and places that make up this state offer something special to the country. Together with all the states, Georgia helps make the United States great.

Springer Mountain in Georgia is one end of the Appalachian Trail.

Georgia's roughly 110 miles (177 km) of coastline is known for its beauty.

TIMELINE

1788

Georgia became the fourth state on January 2.

1861

Georgia joined the Southern states to fight in the **American Civil War**.

1886

A scientist from Atlanta named John Pemberton invented Coca-Cola.

1700s 1800s

While living near Savannah, Eli Whitney invented the cotton gin. This machine made cleaning cotton easier.

1793

Atlanta was named Georgia's **capital**.

1868

1912

Juliette Gordon Low started the first US Girl Guides troop in Savannah. This later became the Girl Scouts.

2011

A set of tornadoes hit Georgia and several nearby states. It was the largest set ever recorded. It destroyed towns and caused many deaths.

2017

Atlanta United FC became a Major League Soccer team.

1900s

2000s

Atlanta hosted the Summer Olympics.

1996

The Atlanta Falcons football team played in the Super Bowl. They lost to the New England Patriots.

2017

TOUR BOOK

Do you want to go to Georgia? If you visit the state, here are some places to go and things to do!

VIEW

Georgia's tallest mountain peak is Brasstown Bald. It is 4,784 feet (1,458 m) tall. From the top, you can see much of the Blue Ridge Mountains.

CHEER

Catch an Atlanta Braves baseball game at SunTrust Park!

Chipper Jones was a star player for the Braves for 19 seasons. He retired in 2012.

DISCOVER

Learn about life under the sea at the Georgia Aquarium. This is the nation's largest aquarium. It opened in Atlanta in 2005.

This aquarium is the only one outside Asia that has whale sharks!

LEARN

Visit the Fernbank Museum of Natural History in Atlanta. It is home to the Argentinosaurus, the world's largest known dinosaur!

REMEMBER

Visit one of Georgia's historic plantation homes. These were large working farms around the time of the American Civil War.

FAST FACTS

▶ STATE FLOWER
Cherokee Rose

▶ STATE TREE
Live Oak

▶ STATE BIRD
Brown Thrasher

▶ STATE FLAG:

▶ NICKNAMES:
Empire State of the South,
Peach State

▶ DATE OF STATEHOOD:
January 2, 1788

▶ POPULATION (RANK):
10,519,475
(8th most-populated state)

▶ TOTAL AREA (RANK):
59,425 square miles
(24th largest state)

▶ STATE CAPITAL: Atlanta

▶ POSTAL ABBREVIATION:
GA

▶ MOTTO:
"Wisdom, Justice and Moderation"

GLOSSARY

American Civil War—the war between the Northern and Southern states from 1861 to 1865.

capital—a city where government leaders meet.

civil rights movement—the public fight for civil rights for all citizens. Civil rights include the right to vote and freedom of speech.

diverse—made up of things that are different from each other.

Nobel Peace Prize—an award given for helping to make peace in the world.

real estate—the business of selling buildings and land.

region—a large part of a country that is different from other parts.

Revolutionary War—a war fought between England and the North American colonies from 1775 to 1783.

transportation—the act of moving people or things from one place to another.

ONLINE RESOURCES

Booklinks
NONFICTION NETWORK
FREE! ONLINE NONFICTION RESOURCES

To learn more about Georgia, please visit **abdobooklinks.com** or scan this QR code. These links are routinely monitored and updated to provide the most current information available.

INDEX

American Civil War   12, 13, 26, 29

American colonies   12

animals   14, 30

Appalachian Mountains   14

Athens   19

Atlanta   8, 9, 13, 14, 17, 18, 20, 22, 26, 27, 28, 29, 30

Atlantic Ocean   6

Augusta   10, 11, 18

Blue Ridge Mountains   8, 14, 28

Brasstown Bald   28

businesses   8, 16, 17

Carter, Jimmy   22, 23

Chattahoochee River   10

civil rights movement   20, 21

Columbus   9, 11

England   12

Fernbank Museum of Natural History   29

Georgia Aquarium   29

Jones, Chipper   28

King, Martin Luther, Jr.   20, 21

Knight, Gladys   22

Low, Juliette Gordon   27

Martin Luther King Jr. National Historical Park   20

McCoughtry, Angel   18

Native Americans   12

Pemberton, John   26

Plains   22

population   6, 8, 11, 30

Revolutionary War   12

Savannah   26, 27

Savannah River   9

size   6, 30

South (region)   6

Spain   12

statehood   4, 12, 26, 30

US Masters   18

weather   14, 27

Whitney, Eli   26